Grammar**o**polis
PRESENTS

Roger the Pronoun

Written by Coert Voorhees
Illustrations by Powerhouse Animation

Meet the Parts of Speech

I name a specific person, place, thing, or idea. It's a big responsibility, naming things—a responsibility that requires a certain attention to detail.

Nelson the Noun

Some people say I'm all over the place. Some people call me a ball of energy. I take that as a compliment, because I just like to go, go, go!

Vinny the Action Verb

I take the place of one or more Nouns or Pronouns. I always want the Noun's job, and I hang out with the Verb and Adjective.

Roger the Pronoun

I'm perfectly happy to link Nouns and Pronouns with the appropriate Adjectives, but it's not like I'm going to expend a lot of energy doing so.

Lucy the Linking Verb

I modify a Noun or Pronoun. I tell what kind, which one, how many, or how much. I pride myself on being the most artistic of the parts of speech.

Jake the Adjective

Gather 'round everybody and let's have ourselves a wonderful time. I just love bringing words and groups of words together, don't you?

Connie the Conjunction

I modify a Verb, Adjective, or other Adverb. I tell how, when, where, to what extent, and under what condition. I often end in –ly, but I don't have to.

Benny the Adverb

I express emotion!! Yep, I'm always here, always ready with my commas and exclamation points, just in case.

Izzy the Interjection

They call me Preposition because I'm pre-positioned. I'm first. At the front. Before every other word in the phrase? Got it?

Li'l Pete the Preposition

I am a chameleon. A spy. An undercover operative. I infiltrate the sentence and act as whatever part of speech suits me.

Slang

ROGER THE PRONOUN

© 2019 Grammaropolis

Graphic Design by Mckee Frazior
Printed by Friesens, Altona, Manitoba, Canada

Text and Illustrations © 2011 by Grammaropolis LLC

This book is typeset in Komika Text

Distributed throughout the world
by Ingram Publisher Services
www.ingrambook.com

Printed in Canada

Roger the pronoun usually spent most of his day with Nelson.

A pronoun's job was to take the place of one or more nouns or pronouns.

If Roger wasn't paying attention, the pronoun wouldn't agree with the word it replaced, called the "antecedent."

Everyone loved Nelson, and Roger was jealous.

He felt he was destined for more.

One night, when he was feeling sad, he practiced his reflexive pronouns. He looked at himself in the mirror.

I need to give myself a pep talk.

The next day, Roger opened up his own shop right below Nelson's Nouns.

NELSON'S
NOUNS

"It" by Roger

Everything ½ off!

SALE

CLEARANCE

Nelson didn't think Roger's idea was a very good one.

NOUNS

"It" by Roger

...thing ½ off!

SALE

CL...ANCE

I don't need antecedents.

But nobody will know what you're talking about!

9

Of course, with no antecedents, Roger's customers were confused.

When Vinny accidentally walked away with something, Roger had to use possessive pronouns.

That's mine.

15

Later, Roger went upstairs to get some advice from Nelson. It didn't seem like anyone was home, so Roger had to use indefinite pronouns.

Hello? Somebody? Anybody?

Benny took Roger downtown, where he questioned him about a possible noun/pronoun disagreement.

What more do you know?

It was Nelson, who had been searching for Roger everywhere.
Oops.
You look tired.
It gets exhausting using only nouns all the time.

Pronouns:
You, me, this, and
that over there

PRONOUNS

A pronoun takes the place of one or more nouns or pronouns.

REPLACING NOUNS

Frederick spilled a jar of mayonnaise on my mother and father.

He spilled it on them.

SUBJECTIVE PERSONAL PRONOUNS

A subjective personal pronoun acts as the subject of the sentence.

You bought all the applesauce in the whole store.

EXAMPLES

I
you
he
she
it
we
they

OBJECTIVE PERSONAL PRONOUNS

An objective personal pronoun acts as the object of a verb, preposition, or infinitive phrase.

EXAMPLES: me, you, her, him, it, us, them

Reggie threw me a bag of nachos.

Indirect object of the verb threw.

Vinny and Lucy invited us to the play!

Direct object of the verb invited.

Izzy did their homework for them.

Object of the preposition for.

The piano was so out of tune that Jake begged Doctor Noize not to play it.

Object of the infinitive phrase to play

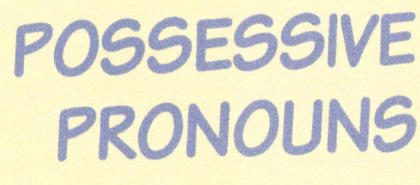

POSSESSIVE PRONOUNS

A possessive pronoun shows ownership or possession.

The computer is *ours*.

Sometimes Patricia likes to take things that are *mine* and not *hers*.

EXAMPLES

mine   yours

his   hers

ours   theirs

INTERROGATIVE PRONOUNS

An interrogative pronoun is used to ask a question. Usually the antecedent is unknown, which is the reason for the question.

What is your name?

Who is your favorite actor?

EXAMPLES

what   who
whom   which
whose

DEMONSTRATIVE PRONOUNS

A demonstrative pronoun replaces one or more nouns and indicates proximity (near or far).

This is Pete's science project.

Those are my shoes.

EXAMPLES

this that
these those

INDEFINITE PRONOUNS

An indefinite pronoun does not refer to a specific noun or pronoun. Often, the antecedent is unknown.

Everyone in this room loves to play Jenga.

Is anybody here?

Pancakes are the best. Please give me another!

EXAMPLES

everyone
anybody
another

An intensive pronoun emphasizes, or intensifies, a noun or another pronoun.

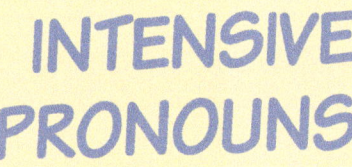

You *yourself* are the biggest goofball in the world.

Yes, I baked all those cookies *myself*.

EXAMPLES

myself   yourself
himself   herself
itself   ourselves
yourselves
themselves

A relative pronoun introduces an adjective clause, which is a subordinate clause that modifies one or more nouns or pronouns.

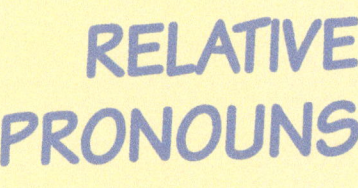

My mother, <u>who is a biologist</u>, loves to scuba dive.

Gerladine prefers chocolate <u>that tastes like raspberries</u>.

EXAMPLES

that which
who whom
whose

CPSIA information can be obtained
at www.ICGtesting.com
Printed in the USA
BVHW050527110519
547997BV00001B/1/P